CloudTrail Event Handling

Common Missteps

Table of Contents

Chapter 1. Introduction

In this Special Report, we delve deep into the often underestimated domain of CloudTrail Event Handling. It's not hyperbolic to state that the ability to properly harness and manage CloudTrail Event Handling can be a game-changer for many businesses. Navigating the multifaceted terrain of such an integral aspect of your cloud computing infrastructure, however, is not without its challenges. Missteps are all too common, yet entirely preventable with a solid understanding of the systems in question. In this comprehensive guide, we've committed ourselves to breaking down these complex technical concepts into practical, digestible pieces. So, whether you're an experienced tech professional aiming to optimize your workflow, or a newcomer looking to avoid the most common pitfalls, this report is a a must-have, offering you significant insights into CloudTrail Event Handling.

Chapter 2. Understanding CloudTrail Event Handling: Basics and Beyond

CloudTrail Event Handling is a fundamental aspect of AWS CloudTrail, a service that provides event history for your AWS account. It helps you to simplify regulatory compliance, security analysis, change tracking, and operational troubleshooting. Whether you are an established professional or new to the field of cloud computing, adopting and mastering this functionality can provide substantial benefits in managing, securing, and optimizing your AWS environments.

2.1. Introduction to AWS CloudTrail

AWS CloudTrail is a service that enables governance, compliance, operational auditing, and risk auditing of your AWS account. By using AWS CloudTrail, you can log, continuously monitor, and retain account activity related to actions across your AWS infrastructure. It provides an event history of your AWS account activity, including actions taken through the AWS Management Console, AWS SDKs, command line tools, and other AWS services.

2.2. Importance of CloudTrail Event Handling

Proper handling of CloudTrail events can provide intelligence businesses can leverage to strengthen security, improve resource management, and make informed decisions. It offers critical insights into who made a call, the source of the call, the services that are invoked, and much more. From a security perspective, CloudTrail

Event logs can be used to identify unusual activity, issue alerts, and in incident response. From an operations point-of-view, they can be helpful in troubleshooting and identifying service inefficiencies for optimization.

2.3. Basics of CloudTrail Event Handling

CloudTrail Event Handling involves dealing with two types of events; management and data events.

Management events provide information about–management operations that are performed on resources in your AWS account. This includes operations such us 'CreateBucket' and 'DeleteSubnet'.

Data Events provide insights about–the resource operations performed on or in a resource itself. These include S3 object-level API operations or Lambdas Invoke API operations.

2.4. Configuring AWS CloudTrail

CloudTrail is enabled on your AWS account when you create it. It delivers a log of management events directly into an Amazon S3 bucket that you specify. You can also configure other AWS services to further analyze and react to CloudTrail events.

To configure\: . Navigate to the CloudTrail console. . In the navigation pane, choose "Trails". . Choose "Create a Trail". . In the "Name" section, specify the name of your trail. . In the "Apply Trail to all Regions" section, choose Yes or No. . In the "Storage Location" section, specify the S3 bucket for your trail logs.

2.5. Analyzing and Understanding CloudTrail Event Data

Analyzing AWS CloudTrail event data effectively requires a well-planned infrastructure for ingesting, parsing, and storing your logs. Once the event data is captured in CloudTrail, it is generally stored in JSON format. Each log consists of several attributes, including event time, user information, source IP addresses, event messages, and others.

AWS provides various services like Amazon Athena, Amazon CloudWatch, and AWS Glue to analyze the event data. It's crucial to understand how to use these services to get the most out of your log data.

2.6. Securing CloudTrail Logs

Using CloudTrail, you can enable log file integrity validation, which allows you to determine whether a log file was modified, deleted, or unchanged after CloudTrail delivered it. To enhance the security of your logs, you can also use Amazon SNS to receive notifications when new log files are delivered, ensuring you have real-time visibility into the activity in your AWS environment.

2.7. Conclusion

AWS CloudTrail event handling is a powerful tool that can provide deep insights into the activity within your AWS environments. However, it requires a good understanding and effective management to fully harness its potential.

This has just been an overview of the immense capabilities of CloudTrail Event Handling. As you dive deeper into this subject, you will unearth a treasure coast of opportunities and solutions to elevate your AWS proficiency, make your operations more secure, resilient, and efficient.

Getting a solid grip on AWS CloudTrail Event handling is not just an add-on to your skills, it is essential for anyone who aspires to manage an AWS environment effectively and professionally. The more you explore, the better your insight will be. Thus, always stay curious, stay updated, and don't forget - every master was once a beginner.

Chapter 3. Common Missteps in CloudTrail Event Handling

Even the most skilled technician can make errors when handling CloudTrail Event Handling, given its complexity and intricacy. These missteps are common and usually echo similar themes. This exploration will focus on uncovering, dissecting, and addressing the most typical mistakes that often take place.

3.1. Failing to Enable CloudTrail

The very first misstep is ironically the most fundamental one - failing to enable CloudTrail. CloudTrail is not activated by default, and an administrator has to manually enable it post creation of an AWS account. This can be overlooked, especially by newcomers, due to lack of awareness or understanding its crucial role in infrastructure security and compliance.

To rectify this, you should ensure CloudTrail is enabled across every region in your AWS environment, regardless of where your assets are currently available. This is because new resources might be added to a different region in the future for load balancing or redundancy purposes, and you want to have logging available from the start.

3.2. Discarding The Management Events Log Files

Another common misstep in CloudTrail Event Handling is overlooking the importance of management events log files. These files carry valuable information on who is making requests on your AWS environment, and more importantly, they provide insights on whether the called API is altering your AWS resources or not.

Ignoring these files blurs visibility into resource modifications, affecting security and compliance efforts. Keeping this log activated and regularly reviewing this is essential to understand who is doing what within your AWS environment.

3.3. Ineffective Log File Validation

CloudTrail log file validation is a robust feature that adds another layer of security to your AWS environment. However, many cloud administrators make the mistake of not enabling and efficiently utilizing this feature.

You see, when an event happens in your account, AWS makes details about this event and then delivers a log file containing those details to your selected S3 bucket. By enabling log file validation, you can automatically detect whether a log file was modified, deleted, or unchanged after CloudTrail delivered it.

Not activating this feature or not paying adequate attention to the alerts and indications of log file validation may lead to delayed detection, or worse, no detection of unauthorized changes, which could have lasting impacts.

3.4. Improper Handling of CloudTrail Logs Storage and Archiving

Due to the sheer volume of logs produced by CloudTrail, some organizations tend to either disregard the storage and archiving of these logs or handle it inefficiently.

Having a thoughtful, dedicated plan for log storage and archiving, considering both the short-term and long-term needs, is crucial not just for operational purposes but also from a security perspective.

Logging the right data, intelligently storing it and setting up archiving rules drastically enhances security, compliance, and analytics capacity.

3.5. Overlooking Multi-Account Trails

Often, organizations handle their cloud environment through multiple AWS accounts for reasons like separating environments, boosting account level security, or facilitating finer control over resources. The logs from these accounts, however, can pile up in their respective S3 buckets, created separately for each account.

This can become an operational nightmare very quickly as you have to individually manage and monitor trails for each account. It is, therefore, advised to set up an organization-level trail that aggregates all these separated trails into a single S3 bucket. Doing so streamlines your CloudTrail Event handling, reduces complexity, and makes event logs easier to parse and analyze.

3.6. Ignoring Multiple Role-based Access

Lastly, it is important to enforce and check for the compliance of role-based access. Mismanaging this can lead to unauthorized access to sensitive CloudTrail data.

Create separate roles for different users and accounts and limit access to CloudTrail data based on the principle of least privilege. Monitor compliance with these permissions and carry out regular audits to ensure desired security levels.

In conclusion, handling CloudTrail event logs isn't merely a checkbox activity. It requires strategic planning and constant efforts on monitoring, analysis, and responding to the insights it offers. Avoiding the aforementioned common missteps is the first big stride towards leveraging CloudTrail for enhancing your operational resilience.

Chapter 4. The Importance of Proper Event Configuration

In the ever-evolving sphere of cloud computing, configuring events of the Amazon CloudTrail is a task of paramount importance. It forms the building block of any cloud infrastructure, and its effective implementation ensures seamless operation of your business's digital assets. Configurations establish the rules that govern how your infrastructure responds to various event signals, enabling businesses to harness, diagnose, and resolve event-related issues effectively.

4.1. Understanding Event Configuration

CloudTrail Event Configuration is essentially the predefined ruleset dictating how different activity on your AWS resources is managed. Imagine being a signal manager at a large railway network. Your role involves making sure everything is running smoothly, monitoring signals, and controlling switches. Now, event configuration is somewhat akin to this scenario, where you control and oversee the cloud 'traffic', making sure all the components of your infrastructure communicate efficiently.

When we discuss 'events', it is in the context of changes or updates that occur to your resources held in AWS. Each event generates a log, a sort of digital footprint. The configuration of these events basically means telling CloudTrail what events you wish to track and manage, creating a framework that allows for optimal resource usage and proactive troubleshooting.

4.2. Why Is Event Configuration Crucial?

To put it simply, event configuration answers two crucial questions—'what happened?' and 'when did it happen?' With correctly configured CloudTrail, businesses can tap into a wealth of data relating to all the changes on their AWS resources. This empowers organizations to adapt rapidly and handle issues before they become major obstacles, aiding in reducing downtime and promoting operational efficiency.

Three primary reasons illustrate why proper event configuration is so critical for enterprises:

1) Security: With AWS CloudTrail, you get an eagle-eye view into user activity and resource usage. This event visibility serves as a valuable security instrument detecting unauthorized access to resources, identifying vulnerabilities, and maintaining regulatory compliance.

2) Operational Troubleshooting: CloudTrail allows operators to trace back operational issues right up to their root cause. When this is combined with other AWS tools like CloudWatch, you get yourself a potent diagnostic tool that can even suggest preventive and corrective measures.

3) Compliance: CloudTrail event logs are invaluable for auditing. They provide a way to review changes to your AWS resources and verify adherence to strict industrial and internal compliance.

4.3. Configuring AWS CloudTrail Events

Configuring AWS CloudTrail involves creating and setting up a trail — essentially a configuration that specifies where, how, and which events you want to log. Trails can be set to apply to all regions or specific ones, with delivery options to a dedicated S3 bucket.

Let's guide you through the steps of setting up your first trail:

1) Navigate to the CloudTrail console in AWS. 2) Click on 'Create trail'. 3) In the 'Trail name', give a unique identifier to your trail.

Next, you move onto selecting what events the trail will log:

1) There are three primary types of events: Management events, Data events, and Insights events. Management events entail actions that are performed on resources, like deletion or alteration. Data events cover activities within the resource itself, and Insight events handle unusual call patterns to aid in the identification of potential issues. 2) In the 'Apply trail to all regions' option, choose whether you want your trail to apply to all regions or to a specific region.

Finally, select where your logs will be delivered:

1) Choose to create a new S3 bucket or select an existing one where your logs will be deposited. 2) Click on 'Create' to finalize your trail.

Once this is done, AWS CloudTrail will start logging events as per your trail definition. You can change the rules/configuration of your trail anytime from the CloudTrail console page under the 'Trails' section.

4.4. Best Practices for Amazon CloudTrail Event Configurations

Adhering to best practices when configuring CloudTrail events will prove beneficial for your infrastructure in the long run. Here are some universally accepted practices:

1) Always Enable Logging in All Regions: This safeguards your

resources, even if they are relocated or launched accidentally or maliciously in another region. 2) Use Multi-region Trails: Multi-region trails allow for the tracking of events regardless of the region of the target resource. This ensures that you get a comprehensive account of activities across your infrastructure. 3) Have More than One Trail with Different S3 Buckets: Segregation of logs in different buckets for different trails provides an added layer of security. Even if one trail is compromised, the others can still provide you with valuable data. 4) Encrypt Log Files with AWS KMS: AWS Key Management Service (KMS) helps in the safe encryption of your log files. 5) Regularly Monitor and Review Your Trails: Regular checks on the health and functioning of your trails provide invaluable insights and opportunities to correct any misconfigurations early on.

In conclusion, consequential as AWS CloudTrail event configurations are, it is vital to not only grasp their importance, but also master their handling. A well-configured CloudTrail setup forms a fundamental block to an effective and secure AWS architecture. Ultimately, harnessing the power of CloudTrail event configurations is all about preserving an organization's agility in the face of swiftly changing business scenarios.

Chapter 5. Streamlining CloudTrail Logging

From the moment an AWS account is created, CloudTrail is automatically activated. This means that every event that happens within your AWS environment is logged and stored. But all this data can be overwhelming and hard to manage without a proper strategy in place. The following sections will provide a deep dive into how you can streamline your CloudTrail logging in order to ensure that your AWS environment remains secure, efficient, and effective.

5.1. Understanding Your Logging Needs

Before we begin optimizing your CloudTrail Logging, we need to understand what your logging requirements are. These requirements can vary depending on your organizational size, industry regulations, and the complexity of your AWS environment. Take some time to understand the legislation that your industry may be subject to, i.e., GDPR, CCPA, HIPAA, etc. Meeting these requirements often means retaining logs for a mandated period.

5.2. Configuring CloudTrail Event Logging

The first step in managing your CloudTrail logs is setting up your event logging preferences. AWS allows you to choose between management events, data events, and insights events. Management events relate to operations performed on resources in your AWS account. Data events pertain to API activities initiated by or upon resources, such as S3 bucket object-level operations. Insight events, the newest addition, help identify unusual operational activity patterns. Understanding the distinction between these categories will guide the configuration process and ensure you're logging the most meaningful data.

5.3. Optimizing Event Selection

Generally, it's best to log all management events as they provide high-level operational details. However, data events can increase costs, so selective logging based on your requirements is suggested to balance cost and information needs. S3 bucket and Lambda function data events are billed separately, and turning on insight events involves an additional cost. Thus, ensure only necessary API activity is tracked.

5.4. Aggregating and Separating Logs

To understand activity across your entire AWS organization, aggregate logs across all accounts and regions in one S3 bucket. This repository can serve as a single source of auditing. However, be aware that this may potentially result in large amounts of data, so proper indexing is key.

For sensitive accounts or very active regions, you may wish to separate logs to reduce the chance of accidental deletion or overwriting. By doing so, you're building a security model around your logs that matches your AWS resource usage.

5.5. Log File Validation

CloudTrail provides log file integrity validation. This important mechanism helps determine if a log file was modified, deleted, or unchanged after CloudTrail delivered it. This feature affirms that the events captured in your logs are as they occurred, offering a chain of custody for audit procedures.

5.6. Long-term Storage with Glacier

For long-term storage, particularly for compliance purposes, consider using Amazon Glacier. It is a low-cost, secure and durable storage service. Transitioning your log files automatically to Amazon Glacier after a predefined period can help you meet data durability, retention, and security requirements.

5.7. Integrating with CloudWatch

For a real-time solution, consider integrating CloudTrail with CloudWatch. CloudWatch alarms can notify you of specific API activity. You can even create custom metrics for specific types of API calls. With CloudWatch metrics and alarms in place, you can react promptly and mitigate potential issues.

5.8. Routing Logs to ElasticSearch

ElasticSearch provides an effective way to analyze CloudTrail logs. AWS Lambda can transform and ship your CloudTrail logs to ElasticSearch. It not only helps you visualize but also allows you to create comprehensive dashboards from your logs.

5.9. Automating through Lambda Functions

AWS Lambda functions offer a serverless way to process your CloudTrail logs automatically. Depending upon the event observed, you can define trigger-based actions in response. From shutting down EC2 instances running in odd hours to denying unauthorized access attempts - automatic action can secure your AWS resources seamlessly.

Streamlining CloudTrail logging not only ensures efficient logging but also helps in monitoring, managing costs, fault-diagnosis, ensuring compliance, and swiftly mitigating any security threats. The scalability of the AWS environment mandates such thorough processing and scrutiny of logs. Remember, effective logging is a recurring cycle rather than a 'set and forget' task. Constant refinement based on varied factors is not only desirable but crucial for a robust AWS environment.

Chapter 6. Proactive Measures: Identifying and Preventing Common Errors

Proactive measures involve a two-pronged approach: identifying potential errors before they occur and taking steps to prevent them from happening in the future. As they say in the world of IT, prevention is always better than cure. So, let's dive in and help you better navigate your way through CloudTrail Event Handling.

6.1. Identification of Common Errors

Understanding the most common errors that occur in the field of CloudTrail Event Handling is the first step to proactive prevention.

Error 001: Misconfigured Monitoring

An all-too-common error is misconfigured monitoring. This can occur when event selectors are not properly configured or when logging is turned off in some or all regions. If CloudTrail logging is not enabled in every region where AWS services are used, you will not have a complete picture of all events.

In asciidoc syntax, here is an example of how to check whether CloudTrail is enabled in all regions:

```
GetTrailStatusCommandExample {
   Name: 'my-trail-name',
}
```

Error 002: Lack of Log File Integrity Validation

Not enabling log file integrity validation is another trap some organizations fall into. Without integrity validation, you cannot have an added layer of security that ensures log files have not been tampered with.

Error 003: Inadequate Data Retention and Storage Policy

An inadequate data retention and storage policy, or DRSP, is another potential source of problems. The most common issue here is not storing CloudTrail logs for a sufficient period of time to meet auditing requirements.

6.2. Preventing Common Errors

The other part of our proactive measures approach is preventing common errors from happening. Now that we know the common errors that can occur, let's look at how we can prevent them.

Prevention Measure for Error 001: Correct Configuration of Monitoring

The first step in preventing misconfigured monitoring is to enable CloudTrail in all regions where AWS services are used. Make sure to include global service events. Additionally, event selectors must be properly configured to record both management and data events.

In AsciiDoc syntax, here is how to enable CloudTrail in all regions:

```
CreateTrailCommandExample {
  Name: 'my-trail-name',
  IncludeGlobalServiceEvents: true
}
```

Prevention Measure for Error 002: Enable Log File Validation

To prevent the second error, navigate to the 'Create Trail' page on your AWS management console and enable log file integrity validation.

In AsciiDoc syntax:

```
CreateTrailCommandExample {
  Name: 'my-trail-name',
  EnableLogFileValidation: true
}
```

Prevention Measure for Error 003: Implement A Data Retention Plan

When it comes to preventing an inadequate data retention and storage policy, the answer lies in putting a thorough system in place. This should include timely reviews and regular updates of your storage requirements, and ensuring those requirements align with your organization's policies and any legal obligations.

In AsciiDoc syntax, here is how to set a log retention period of 365 days:

```
CreateTrailCommandExample {
  Name: 'my-trail-name',
  BucketName: 'my-AWSBucket',
  S3KeyPrefix: 'AWSLogs',
  LogFileValidationEnabled: true,
  CloudWatchLogsLogGroupArn: 'my-LogGroupArnModel',
  CloudWatchLogsRoleArn: 'my-RoleArnModel',
  KmsKeyId: 'my-KmsKeyIdModel',
  IsOrganizationTrail: true,
  IsMultiRegionTrail: true,
```

```
    IncludeGlobalServiceEvents: true,
    IsLogging: true,
    SnsTopicName: 'my-SnsTopicModel',
}
```

By identifying potential problems before they occur, and establishing measures to prevent them, we can avoid many common errors and issues in CloudTrail Event Handling. Remember, being proactive is better than being reactive in the world of IT. Having a clear understanding of these proactive measures, and applying them diligently, will be key to harnessing the full potential of CloudTrail Event Handling.

Coming up, we'll talk about the best practices for handling CloudTrail Events. These best practices, when applied consistently, will help you ensure that your AWS environment is both secure and efficient.

We hope this chapter helps in your journey to perfect CloudTrail event handling. While we've covered some of the biggest common errors that can occur and how to prevent them, always remember the core principle of IT: "Change is the only constant". As your organization grows and evolves, so too should your preventive measures and action plans. By maintaining a proactive approach and continuously learning and updating your knowledge, you'll ensure that your CloudTrail Event Handling remains robust and efficient, regardless of any challenges thrown your way.

Chapter 7. Advanced Tactics for CloudTrail Troubleshooting

Amazon CloudTrail captures account activity and events in AWS resources and services, hence its troubleshooting can involve a wide range of tactics. Let's delve into how we can troubleshoot CloudTrail effectively using advanced methodologies.

The sections we'll cover in this chapter are:

- Enabling Log File Validation

- CloudTrail Event History Troubleshooting

- Verifying Trail Settings

- Troubleshooting Issues with Delivery

- Understanding CloudTrail Limitations

7.1. Enabling Log File Validation

While AWS tools are reliable most of the time, that doesn't mean they're foolproof. Errors can and do occur occasionally. To ensure the integrity of your CloudTrail logs, you should enable log file validation. It verifies the integrity of the log files delivered by confirming that the log files were unchanged, undamaged, and unaltered.

To enable log file validation, follow the steps below:

1. Navigate to the Trails page in the AWS Management Console.

2. Choose the existing trail.

3. Under 'Log file validation,' click 'YES.'

Remember, a digital signature is then added to the log files. This helps in verifying that an unaltered version of the log is given to your bucket.

7.2. CloudTrail Event History Troubleshooting

While CloudTrail Event History is an excellent tool to check and analyze account-level activity, there might arise situations where specific events are missing or unnoticed. Here are a few things to consider while troubleshooting Event History:

- The event being looked up for is a 'management event.' Data events and insights events are not recorded in the Event history.

- The event was taken within the last 90 days. CloudTrail Event history only retains these records within 90 days.

If you need to store logs for extended periods or need data and insights events, consider creating a trail in CloudTrail.

7.3. Verifying Trail Settings

While setting the trails, some configurations must be accurately done to ensure information flow. If you're missing particular logs or not seeing the logs you need in your S3 bucket, it might be due to incorrect trail settings.

To verify your trail settings:

1. Go to AWS Management Console → CloudTrail → Trails.

2. Select the trail to verify its settings.

3. In the trail settings, you should look for "S3 bucket" for log delivery and "CloudWatch Logs log group" for CloudWatch delivery.

Verify that events are being logged to where you expect and that all the required services, global services, and regions are included in your trail.

7.4. Troubleshooting Issues with Delivery

If the delivery of your CloudTrail log files to your specified destination (typically an Amazon S3 bucket) is inconsistent or failing, you should verify the permissions on your bucket policies, bucket ACLs, and IAM user policies.

You should also check if your bucket policy enables proper write privileges to CloudTrail. You need to include the following statement:

```
{
    "Sid": "AWSCloudTrailWrite20131101",
    "Effect": "Allow",
    "Principal": {"Service":
"cloudtrail.amazonaws.com"},
    "Action": "s3:PutObject",
    "Resource":
"arn:aws:s3:::<YOUR_BUCKET_NAME>/AWSLogs/<YOUR_ACCOUNT>/
CloudTrail/*",
    "Condition": {"StringEquals": {"s3:x-amz-acl":
"bucket-owner-full-control"}}
}
```

This IAM policy ensures that your CloudTrail logs can be delivered effectively to your S3 bucket without any permissions-related issues.

7.5. Understanding CloudTrail Limitations

Knowing how CloudTrail functions and its limitations can assist you in troubleshooting problem areas effectively:

- Events might not appear in the exact order they occur.

- Some types of events are logged by default, while others are not.

- The number of trails per region and the number of events per API call have limits.

In conclusion, CloudTrail is an invaluable piece of your AWS toolbox, allowing for improved visibility and efficiency across your infrastructure. By implementing these tactics, you can ensure that you maximize these benefits while minimizing issues. Effective troubleshooting will help you detect anomalies in your system and respond to them swiftly, leading to a safer, more reliable AWS environment.

Chapter 8. Securing Your CloudTrail Events: Best Practices

In today's fast-paced and constantly evolving digital world, the security of complex computing systems is a top priority. One area within this system where security is of utmost importance is in CloudTrail Event Handling. Here, we discuss best practices for securing your CloudTrail events.

First, it's important to ensure that CloudTrail is enabled in all regions. This not only broadens coverage, but also prevents the possibility of missing out on crucial events occurring outside of priorly mapped regions.

`[source,]

```
aws cloudtrail describe-trails
----`

This is the command you would use to check if CloudTrail
is enabled in all regions. If not, you can use the
following command:

`[source,]
```

aws cloudtrail create-subscription --name AllRegionTrail --s3-new-bucket mybucket ----`

In this, replace 'mybucket' with your preferred bucket name to enable CloudTrail in all regions.

8.1. Ensuring Log File Validation

Next, log file validation is another essential measure to ensure the integrity and accuracy of your event data. Enabling log file validation helps in determining whether or not a log file was tampered before delivery to the specified S3 bucket.

`[source,]

```
aws cloudtrail update-trail --name trailname --enable
-log-file-validation
----`


Change 'trailname' to your specified CloudTrail's name
to enable log file validation.


=== Encryption


Coming to the matter of encryption, AWS key management
service (KMS) should be leveraged to encrypt CloudTrail
log files. The following command will enable encryption:


`[source,]
```

aws cloudtrail update-trail --name trailname --kms-key-id alias/keyname ----`

Replace 'trailname' and 'keyname' with your appropriate trail name and key name, respectively.

8.2. Creating a CloudWatch Alarm

Detecting unauthorized activity early is also pivotal. Creating a CloudWatch Alarm for changes in your CloudTrail configurations will allow you to receive SNS notifications for any alteration.

`[source,]

```
cloudwatch set-alarm-state --alarm-name "Your
configuration changes" --state-reason "Unauthorized API
activity detected" --state-value ALARM
----`


Replace 'Your configuration changes' with your chosen
alarm name to set up this feature.

=== Implement Access Control Lists

Controlling who can access your S3 bucket where
CloudTrail logs are stored is crucial. Implementing
Access Control Lists (ACLs) can help in defining user-
specific permissions.

`[source,]
```

aws s3api put-bucket-acl --bucket mybucket --acl private ----`

Replace 'mybucket' with your chosen bucket name. This command
will limit all access to bucket owners only.

8.3. Restricting Access by Creating Bucket Policies

You can restrict access by creating bucket policies. Remember to
grant read permissions to AWS CloudTrail's AWS accounts.

`[source,]

```json
{
    "Version": "2012-10-17",
    "Id": "Policy1415115909153",
    "Statement": [
        {
            "Sid": "Allow CloudTrail to deliver logs",
            "Principal": { "Service":
"cloudtrail.amazonaws.com" } ,
            "Effect": "Allow",
            "Action": "s3:PutObject",
            "Resource":
"arn:aws:s3:::bucket_name/AWSLogs/account_id/*",
            "Condition": { "StringEquals": { "s3:x-amz-
acl": "bucket-owner-full-control" } }
        }
    ]
}
----`
```

Don't forget to replace 'bucket_name' with your specific
bucket name and 'account_id' with your unique AWS
account ID.

CloudTrail Event Handling is a powerful tool when
implemented correctly and securely. By following these
best practices, you ensure the integrity, accuracy, and
security of your event data, thus enhancing the overall
functionality of your cloud computing system. The world
of cloud computing carries many potential complexities,
but with a solid understanding, this terrain becomes
much more navigable.

== Making Use of CloudTrail Event History
AWS CloudTrail is the go-to service for AWS management
events, data events, and CloudTrail Insights events,

meticulously tracking every activity that happens within
your AWS environment. By making judicious use of
CloudTrail's Event History, you tap into a goldmine of
information that can drive performance enhancement
decisions, fortify security, and ramp up debugging
efficiency.

=== Understanding Raw Event Data

Understanding raw event data sits at the forefront of
effective CloudTrail event handling. An event, by AWS
definition, encapsulates a single instance of activity
within your AWS environment. Every action that's taken
through AWS Management Console, AWS Software Development
Kits (SDKs), command line tools, and other AWS services,
generates an event.

In its raw form, each event is a JSON-formatted document
containing an array of information about the parent
activity. Scroll through an event document and you'll
find key data points such as the event name, AWS region,
source IP address, resources affected, and much more.
Harnessing this raw information, to the untrained eye,
is a daunting task.

However, events are stored in AWS CloudTrail by default
for 90 days, but you can greatly extend this through
CloudTrail trails, storing data in a designated Amazon
S3 bucket or a CloudWatch Logs log group. This allows
you to have a considerable amount of data to work with
for audit, operational troubleshooting, or compliance
needs.

=== Interpreting Event History

To interpret your Event History and correlate events

effectively, you need to familiarize yourself with critical event attributes. The 'eventTime' signifies when the occurrence took place. The 'eventSource' reveals the AWS service responsible for the event. The 'eventName' provides insights into what action was performed. The 'userIdentity' segment offers a look into who initiated the action, delving into the IAM role, user, and other details. The 'errorCode' and 'errorMessage', if present, give quick insights into what went wrong in case of a failed event.

Looking beyond individual event records, CloudTrail aggregates common patterns into Insights events, which are designed to make it easier for you to identify unusual activities, such as sudden spikes in resource provisioning, API call rates, or even unauthorized user behavior scenarios.

=== Decoding with CloudTrail Lookup API

To step up your event handling, CloudTrail Lookup API comes into play. This API lets you explore, analyze, and report on the user activity captured in your Event History. Look up events within a specified date and time range and slice and dice the data based on key attributes. AWS SDKs and AWS CLI support CloudTrail Lookup APIs for programmatic access to lookup and filter events.

Note that CloudTrail Lookup API does adhere to strict request limits. Exceed these limits, and API requests will be throttled, with error messages thrown in response.

=== Implementing Effective Auditing with Event History

Audit logging is the bread and butter of any diligent
AWS ecosystem monitoring attempt. CloudTrail's Event
History, armed with all the useful event data, makes
auditing relatively straightforward. Revisit any
activity, verify compliance, detect anomalies,
troubleshoot issues, and conduct security assessments
with ease.

To streamline your auditing efforts, consider routing
your CloudTrail events into Amazon CloudWatch Logs. This
lets you monitor system, application, and custom logs in
real time - delivering instant auditing capabilities.
Set up alarms to alert you of any suspicious behaviors,
error code influxes, and more.

=== Making Use of Advanced Event Selectors in Trails

If you need to capture events related to a specific
resource or a set of resources, you can make use of
advanced event selectors in your CloudTrail trails.
These selectors allow you to include or exclude AWS API
calls that are made to specific resources. Be aware that
event selection, particularly involving data events,
counts towards your monthly allotment and can reflect on
your AWS bill.

All told, CloudTrail Event History offers a trove of
data that, when correctly interpreted and efficiently
used, can significantly bolster the operational
transparency of your AWS environment. Whether you're
focused on auditing, troubleshooting, compliance, or
security insights, the Event History has you covered
with an impressive array of tools and actionable data.

== Customizing CloudTrail to Fulfill Business Needs
Amazon Web Services (AWS) CloudTrail is a web service

that enables governance, compliance, operational auditing, and risk assessment of your AWS activity. But, simply utilizing these services without customization may not yield the optimal results for your business needs. A thorough, refined approach which encompasses customizing CloudTrail to suit your unique requirements can vastly enhance your operational efficiency and mitigate potential risks.

Let's dive into how you can specifically tailor CloudTrail to fulfill your business needs.

=== Understanding the Basics

Firstly, understanding how AWS CloudTrail operates is fundamental. It records AWS API calls for your account and delivers the log files to you. The recorded information consists of the identity of the API caller, the time of the API call, the source IP address of the API caller, the request parameters, and the response elements returned by the AWS service. These logs enable you to perform security analysis, resource change tracking, and compliance auditing.

=== Customizing Log File Delivery

AWS CloudTrail provides two ways to get log files: get log files delivered to a specified S3 bucket (the default option), or have CloudTrail publish CloudWatch Logs events for each API call. However, you might want to customize the delivery to satisfy other specific business requirements. This could involve using multiple trails, multiple S3 buckets, or customizing the log file aggregation by regions or accounts.

=== Using Multiple Trails

While a single trail can be efficient, multiple trails can provide several advantages. For instance, you could segment data based on the sensitivity level or department, creating a separate trail for each. The number of trails you need will depend on how granular you want your segmentation to be for auditing purposes.

=== Using Multiple S3 Buckets

Deploying multiple S3 buckets allows you to store log files in different containers based on your preference. You could store logs from different trails or regions in separate buckets. Partitioning your logs like this can improve organization and accessibility, and may also help with compliance and auditing activities.

=== Log File Aggregation

You may want to consider aggregating log files across regions or accounts. For example, you could choose to receive log files from all regions in a central Amazon S3 bucket. This dramatically simplifies management and auditing. You also could configure CloudTrail to deliver log files from multiple accounts to a single S3 bucket. This enables easy cooperation between accounts, and enhances overall security.

=== Advanced Customizations

Once the basics are covered, there are further customizations you might perform: integrating with CloudWatch for real-time monitoring, enabling encryption with KMS, setting up log file integrity validation, and extending log file retention by integrating CloudTrail with Lifecycle policies.

=== Integrating with CloudWatch

By integrating with CloudWatch, you get real-time
monitoring capabilities - a significant advantage when
troubleshooting events. You can set alarms to notify you
when specific events occur, offering you more control
over your AWS environment.

=== Enabling Encryption with KMS

By default, CloudTrail log files are encrypted using
Amazon S3 Server Side Encryption (SSE). But for a higher
level of security and control, you might want to enable
KMS encryption. KMS encryption enables management of
cryptographic keys, which can be used to secure your
data.

=== Log File Integrity Validation

Enabling log file validation ensures that the delivered
log files have not been tampered with. By hashing and
delivering a digest file along with the logs, the
integrity of the records can be validated at any time –
a crucial feature for maintaining a strong security
posture.

=== Lifecycle Policies

By integrating with Lifecycle policies, you can manage
the retention and expiration of your log files. This
feature allows a streamlined approach to managing older
files and can aid in reducing storage costs.

By understanding and implementing these customizations
effectively, you can make AWS CloudTrail an even more

valuable resource for your organization. This, in turn,
aids in the improvement of your overall cloud computing
operations, honing the ability to control and secure
your environment effectively.

== Harnessing the Power of CloudTrail Monitoring
CloudTrail, AWS's answer to auditing, provides a
valuable record of the action history within an AWS
environment. Effective monitoring of these records can
enable a more secure, efficient, and compliant cloud
ecosystem. In this guide, we'll explore in detail how to
harness this incredibly versatile tool—or rather,
service—offered by AWS.

=== Understanding CloudTrail

AWS CloudTrail is a service that enables governance,
compliance, operational auditing, and risk auditing of
your AWS account. By tracking user activity and API
usage, it allows you to ensure accountability, verify
compliance, and pinpoint variances due to human or
mechanical errors.

CloudTrail captures AWS Management Console actions, AWS
SDKs, command-line tools, and other AWS services. The
logged information includes the identity of the API
caller, the time of the API call, the source IP address
of the API caller, the request parameters, and the
response elements returned by the AWS service.

=== Setting Up CloudTrail

Setting up CloudTrail for the first time might appear
daunting. Luckily, creating a trail—a configuration
enabling ongoing delivery of CloudTrail events to an
Amazon S3 bucket—can be accomplished in just a few

steps.

1. Navigate to the CloudTrail console.
2. Choose 'Trails' from the navigation pane.
3. Select ⬚Create trail⬚.
4. For ⬚Trail name⬚, input a name for your trail.
5. In ⬚Management events⬚, choose the ⬚Read/Write events⬚ options fitting your specific needs.
6. For the storage location, input your S3 bucket name.
7. Choose ⬚Create⬚.

=== Leveraging CloudTrail for Audit and Compliance

Through its capabilities of tracking user activity and API usage, CloudTrail has become an indispensable tool for audit and compliance. By examining the information logged by CloudTrail, you can determine the request made to a given service, the IP address the request came from, who made the request, when it was made, and so on.

For instance, you can create an S3 bucket policy that only allows encrypted objects to be uploaded. If the policy is violated, you can use CloudTrail logs to identify the API call that enabled the unencrypted object upload, the IP address where the request came from, and which user made this request.

=== Monitoring Systems with CloudWatch and CloudTrail

This section is concerned with how CloudTrail and CloudWatch, two inherently compatible components of AWS, can be merged to form a powerful, functional amalgamation.

CloudTrail logs can be used in union with Amazon CloudWatch Logs to monitor system-wide activities. By setting an alarm in CloudWatch for specific CloudTrail events, you will receive notifications when certain API activity occurs. Monitoring and alarming on API activity can be indispensable for security and operational purposes.

The integration process is straightforward:

1. Create a new CloudWatch Logs log group.
2. Configure a role for CloudTrail to assume when delivering events to the CloudWatch Logs log group.
3. Configure CloudTrail to send events to the CloudWatch Logs log group.
4. Define metric filters that extract values from CloudTrail events. These allow CloudWatch to alarm and notify based on defined metrics.

=== Fine-Tuning CloudTrail Logging

CloudTrail has been designed to accommodate systems of different scales and complexity, serving a wide array of industries. As such, it can be finely tuned to fit specific requirements, leading to significant performance improvements and cost savings.

You can choose to include or exclude management and data events or select specific S3 buckets or Lambda functions to monitor. You can also include or exclude global services, services in other regions, or all read and write API events in your logging.

While setting up these configurations, it's important to weigh the costs (both financial and performance-related) against the potential gains in security, monitoring, and compliance. In doing so, your CloudTrail setup will reflect both your operational needs and your budget.

=== Conclusion

Without doubt, harnessing CloudTrail and mastering its intricacies, opens up an expansive playing field for enhancing your system's monitoring, security, operational auditing, and risk auditing. By understanding the functionality of CloudTrail, and interlinking it with other AWS services like CloudWatch, you can build a robust, secure, and efficient AWS ecosystem. With the right configurations and fine-tuning, the advantages of this powerhouse resource are just a trail away. Now, the next steps, applying this knowledge and experience, are in your capable hands.